KNOWLEDGE ENCYCLOPEDIA
ANCIENT & MEDIEVAL ART

© Wonder House Books 2025

All rights reserved. No part of this book may be reproduced or transmitted in any form by any means, electronic or mechanical, including photocopying and recording, or by any information storage and retrieval system except as may be expressly permitted in writing by the publisher.

(An imprint of Prakash Books)

contact@wonderhousebooks.com

Disclaimer: The information contained in this encyclopedia has been collated with inputs from subject experts. All information contained herein is true to the best of the Publisher's knowledge.

ISBN : 9789390391400

Table of Contents

Ageless Art	3
Prehistoric Art	4–5
Mesopotamian Marvels	6–7
Astounding Egypt	8–9
Ancient Persia	10–11
Minoa and Mycenae	12–13
Archaic, Classical, and Hellenistic Greece	14–15
Art of the Roman Empire	16–17
Medieval Islam	18–19
South Asian Art	20–21
Imperial China	22–23
Japanese Art	24–25
The Amazing Americas	26–27
Medieval Europe	28–29
Masterpieces of the Dark Ages	30–31
Word Check	32

AGELESS ART

Human beings are social animals. For us, it is essential to express our thoughts and emotions. Art is both a basic and sophisticated form of expression. Even before they invented writing, ancient people were using their fingers and bone fragments, as well as brushes, to scribble down their thoughts in pictures and symbols. Images were also carved into ivory and antlers. These ancient forms of art soon developed in complexity. They extended to other materials, such as paintings on pottery, silk and paper, sculpture, and metalwork. Over the centuries, art has become a part of rituals and ceremonies, an outlet for the imagination, a vehicle for social justice, and even a form of entertainment.

▼ The Moai statues are giant human figures carved from single blocks of stone by the aboriginal people of Easter Island

Prehistoric Art

The earliest examples of human art date from times of myth and mystery. In Africa, Asia, Europe, and South America, art has been discovered from people who lived 40,000 years ago. Such sculptures and paintings are in secluded spots like caves, away from the destructive wind, rain, and new life.

▲ The Stone Age rock art at Bhimbetka caves shows the earliest signs of human life on the Indian subcontinent

Meaning

Hundreds of prehistoric artworks were sheltered from the open air or hidden away in remote places. These are still around today. They show us what ancient human beings thought, felt, and believed. They show an eternal yearning for beauty, for belonging, and for spiritual meaning.

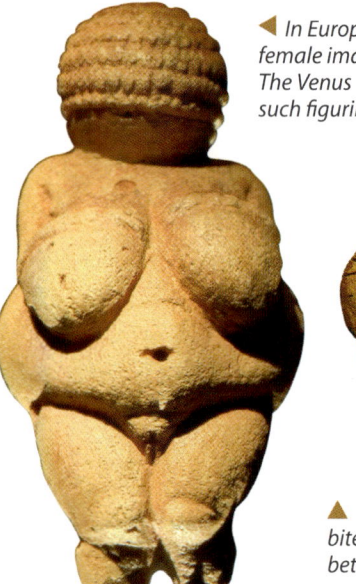

◀ In Europe, over the period 30,000–20,000 BCE, female images of all ages were created in abundance. The Venus of Willendorf is the most famous among such figurines

▲ The prehistoric site of Stonehenge in England is a famous circle of menhirs (long upright stones). Other such arrangements of ancient human-made blocks of stone can be seen across Europe

▲ This figure of a bison licking an insect bite was carved from the antler of a reindeer between 20,000 and 12,000 BCE in France

Cave Art

We tend to think of the Stone Age as a time when human societies were basic. But the artworks from this time show us otherwise. In Europe and Africa, the caves where hunter-gatherers lived are covered with paintings, engravings, and low **relief sculptures**. They show hunting packs of humans, fierce animals, and mysterious symbols. Even back then, artists knew to exaggerate certain elements to show a subject's innermost nature. Mammoths and rhinos were drawn with formidable tusks and horns. Horses and deer seemed to move like the wind. Mythical beasts including half-animal, half-human creatures were also created. Portraits of people were rare.

▶ In the rock paintings of Manda Guéli Cave in Central Africa, camels have been painted over earlier images of cattle. This is perhaps a reflection of the changing climate

ANCIENT & MEDIEVAL ART

Stone Age Animals

Ancient artworks allow us to see what fearsome and spectacular animals lived during the long Stone Age period. These include the cave lion, ancient bears, the woolly rhinoceros, the sabre-toothed tiger, the mammoth, the giant deer, and the large-horned buffalo. The animals drawn most often were the ones considered useful. In European cave art, for instance, horses, bison, reindeer, aurochs, wild boar, fish, eels, and birds were drawn. They were valued for food, fur, leather, and bone. In Africa, people painted animals in natural combinations like herds of giraffes and elephants, or lakes with hippopotami, crocodiles, and birds.

Isn't It Amazing!

Not all cave art was done by hand. Sometimes a piece of carved bone would be used to create a piece of art. The Lascaux Cave of France was painted with a wonderful tool specific to artists—paint brushes made of animal fur. Another tool was the *burin*, which was a chisel-like piece of rock used to make engravings on stone, which helped even nomadic people make portable art.

▲ *Bisons at Altamira Cave, in Spain*

▲ *Tin Taghirt in Algeria has exquisite rock carvings; among them is a sleeping antelope and a now extinct buffalo-like animal*

Thought and Art

Ideograms are shapes or symbols that convey specific ideas. Prehistoric cave paintings contain several such symbols. Amazingly, ancient sites from all across the world show many of the same ideas. They show universal human experience and shared concerns, no matter where people lived. For instance, a handprint on a cave wall might have been a person's way of saying, 'I was here'. The symbols also show how ancient human beings were beginning to convey complex thoughts.

▲ *Prehistoric handprints decorate the Cuevas de las Manos in Argentina*

Practical Art

When ancient human beings began to settle down, they started drawing pictures of their territories on rocks. These early 'maps' showed cultivated fields, the paths to various houses, and landmarks in the neighbourhood. The Topographical Stone of Jebel Amud, in the Jordanian desert, paints a picture of 150 connected settlements. At the Okladnikov cave in Siberia, human figures have been drawn as well—possibly to show a harvest. An ancient wall map in Turkey shows the settlement near an erupting volcano, the first human record of this phenomenon!

▲ *The Bedolina Map at Valcamonica, a valley in Italy, shows some of the most ancient 'maps'*

Mesopotamian Marvels

Mesopotamia is the name given to a vast and ancient land around the rivers Tigris and Euphrates. In modern times, this area covers Iraq and parts of Iran, Turkey, Kuwait, and Syria. Many scholars consider this area to be the birthplace of civilisation. The people who lived in Mesopotamia in ancient times include the Sumerians, Akkadians, Babylonians, and Assyrians. The art of Mesopotamia refers to the art of all these nations. It lasted until Mesopotamia was conquered by the Persian Empire in the 6th century BCE.

Skilled Craftsmen

The most abundant art from Mesopotamia is in the form of pottery and **ceramics**. They were designed with geometric patches and varied in colour. The 6th millennium BCE pottery of Hassuna-Samarra culture shows decorations of human, bird, and animal figures. They are not realistic but stylised figures, emphasising the most attractive features.

In later times, educated people began to use clay reliefs to tell stories. Cylindrical or cubical statues were also developed. Some of the most amazing creations from the 15th century BCE used glass and glazing. The tombs of the rich and the noble at the city of Ur contained beautifully crafted objects of gold, silver, **lapis lazuli**, coloured limestone, and shell. These include jewellery, game-boards, musical harps, weapons, and **seals**.

▲ *This statue of a Sumerian at prayer is made of limestone, alabaster, and shell; it dates back to 2900–2600 BCE*

In Real Life

The earliest known form of nail art dates to ancient Babylonia in around 3200 BCE. At the time, men coloured their nails to show social hierarchy. Upper-class men wore black nail polish and middle-class men wore green. A solid gold manicure set was discovered in a royal tomb in the city of Ur.

▲ *Babylonian men also curled and set their hair with lacquer*

▲ *The Stele of the Vultures narrates the victory of King Eannatum of Lagash over the city Umma, 2540 BCE*

▶ *Ram in a Thicket is the name given to this stunning figurine found at a site called the Great Death Pit of Ur*

◀ *This is one of 26 Sumerian statues of Gudea, ruler of Lagash, crafted in cylindrical and cubical styles, 2100 BCE*

▶ *The Standard of Ur, found in the royal tombs, shows peacetime and is made of lapis lazuli and shell*

Kudurru

The word *kudurru* is an Akkadian term for a boundary. *Kudurrus* are among the few remaining art pieces marking Kassite rule in Babylonia (16th–12th century BCE). To the Kassite people, these carved boundary stones were a common sight, important both in their economics and religion. The purpose of the *kudurru* was to record the grants of land made by a king to someone who had served him well. The original *kudurru* would remain in a temple. Scribes would copy it on to clay slabs and pass on the copy to the landowner. Apart from the actual grant, engraved gods and symbols festooned the *kudurru*. These apparently brought unholy curses on anyone who dared to go against the king.

▶ A kudurru of Marduk-apal-iddina II whose name means 'Marduk has given me an heir.' He was an 8th-century-BCE king of Babylonia who held out against the Assyrian armies for more than a decade

Wartime Art

In the 10th century BCE, the Assyrians battled and took over their neighbouring lands. They rapidly became the dominant force of Mesopotamia. As is common among victors, they proudly recorded their wars and exploits. They used sturdy limestone slabs, detailed carvings, long inscriptions, colourful bricks, and **frescoes**. Metals were used in the form of imposing gates and sculptures. As the Assyrians won campaign after campaign, they brought home treasures from other nations. The loot included numerous artworks, including bronze vessels, furniture and fittings, ivory carvings, and other technically superb and beautiful works.

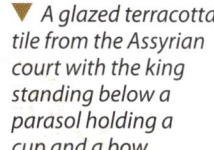

▼ A glazed terracotta tile from the Assyrian court with the king standing below a parasol holding a cup and a bow

▲ An ivory, gold, and lapis lazuli carving of a lion devouring a youth, from Assyrian treasures of 900–700 BCE

▲ Religious art from Dur-Sharrukin (Khorsabad, Iraq) from the palace of Sargon II, King of Assyria (c. 722–705 BCE)

Astounding Egypt

Safe behind its desert borders, ancient Egypt was a thriving civilisation, rich from the fertile land of the Nile. Its wealth and comfort led to the creation of great art forms that served two main purposes. One was spiritual, meant to praise the gods and the Pharaoh, and help people pass into the afterlife. Thus, gods, demons, and mythological beasts were depicted everywhere. The second purpose was to promote Egypt's traditions and values.

▲ Pharaoh is the title of Egypt's divine ruler, who was worshipped as an avatar of the eagle-headed god Horus, seen in this relief at the temple of Set I

▲ The sculpture of Pharaoh Menkaure, with the goddess Hathor and a deity representing the territory of Diospolis Parva

◀ A game board bearing inscriptions of Pharaoh Amenhotep III, 1390–1352 BCE

◀ The iconic funerary mask of King Tutankhamun

Crafts and Jewels

Much of the art left behind by ancient Egyptians comes from their amazing tombs. Egyptian pottery was first made from the clay of the Nile and fired to give blackened tops. Later eras used different clays and greater varieties of decorations. Opaque, bright glass was used for amulets, beads, and small vessels. Coppersmiths made small ornaments out of metal. Craftsmen were also skilled in making fine objects from stone. Lavish jewellery came from semi-precious stones, glass, and precious metals. Apart from gold, stones like turquoise, amethyst, jasper, lapis lazuli, agate, and garnet were greatly coveted.

▲ Winged scarab of Tutankhamun with semi-precious stones

▶ Vessel depicting a galloping horse, New Kingdom of ancient Egypt, 18th dynasty, c. 1340 BCE

ANCIENT & MEDIEVAL ART

Ammut

The demoness Ammut ("the devourer of the dead") had the head of a crocodile, the body of a lion, and the hindquarters of a hippo—all the deadliest man-eaters. She sits by Ma'at (Goddess of Truth), who weighs the hearts of humans on the Scale of Justice. If the heart is as light as a feather, the human is judged to have led a good life. If the heart be heavier, it is devoured by Ammut and the soul is doomed to eternal restlessness!

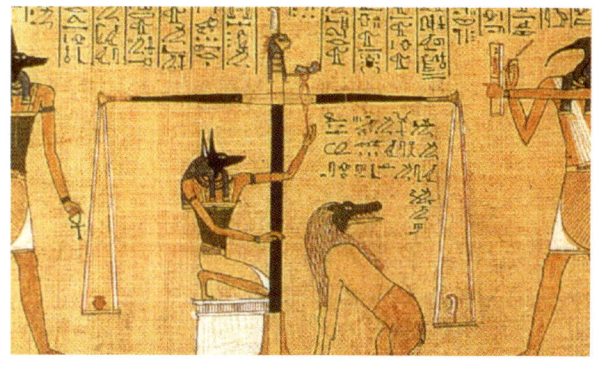

▲ Ma'at, Goddess of Truth, wields the Scale of Justice as the crocodile-headed Ammut waits with an open maw

Faience

Egyptians used a glaze on their pottery made from a ground mineral called quartz. This produced striking blue, green colours and was called *faience*. Faience tiles were used to decorate tombs and palaces. It also produced some of the most amazing jewellery and pottery of the ancient world.

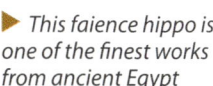

▶ This faience hippo is one of the finest works from ancient Egypt

▶ Lotus-patterned chalice from the 22nd dynasty (945–715 BCE)

▲ A faience wall lamp in the shape of a falcon from the Ptolemaic period, 323–30 BCE

Murals and Paintings

▲ From the Book of the Dead, the jackal-headed god Anubis brings the scribe Hunefer to judgement. Horus then takes him before the god Osiris, seated before his sisters Isis and Nephthys

Egyptian murals are abundant in tombs and palaces. In buildings of mud or brick, murals were painted. The themes varied from myths, legends of royalty and nobility, and the daily lives of the people. Entertaining details and hieroglyphs make these paintings compelling. The invention of papyrus gave Egyptian draftsmen another medium to work with. Papyrus paintings flourished and reached a peak in 1300 BCE. This is represented in the *Book of the Dead*, created by the scribe Ani. In later times, pure line drawings became more popular.

Sphinx

With the body of a lion and the head of a human, the sphinx was first seen in Egyptian lore. In Egyptian art, gods were usually portrayed with human bodies and animal heads. The opposite is true for the sphinx, whose face was usually a royal portrait. Sphinxes even wore the *nemes* (headdress) of a Pharaoh. The female sphinx first appeared in the 15th century BCE.

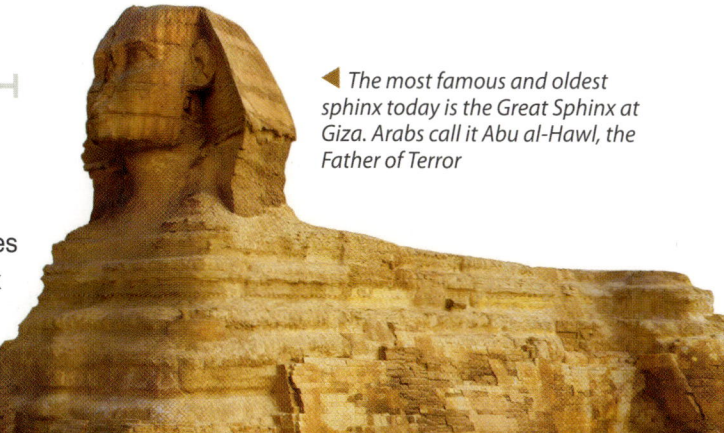

◀ The most famous and oldest sphinx today is the Great Sphinx at Giza. Arabs call it Abu al-Hawl, the Father of Terror

Ancient Persia

The land we now call Iran was historically known as Persia. In its prime, the Persian Empire stretched far beyond modern-day Iran. They were wealthy, influential, and amazingly artistic. The earliest artworks from this region are delicate ceramics from c. 3500 BCE. They belonged to the cities of Susa and Persepolis. Bronze objects from the mountains of Luristan (c. 1200–750 BCE), and a hoard of gold, silver, and ivory from Ziwiye (c. 700 BCE) are some of the other early artworks of ancient Persia.

▲ Pottery from the 4th millennium BCE shows stylised nature, particularly water birds and ibexes (wild goats). They were accompanied by geometrical patterns—a recurring theme in most Persian art

▲ Silver cup from the 3rd millennium BCE

▲ A hammered gold ornament from the Ziwiye hoard showing parades of mythical winged beasts

◀ Luristan bronzes were small, flat, amazing objects. They were fashioned as tools, weapons, horse-ornaments, vessels, finials and so forth

◀ Golden ram-head rhyton (a vessel for drinking)

▲ Forehead ornament for a horse

▲ Silver bowl with gold decorations from Ziwiye

Achaemenian Art

The first powerful Persian empire lasted from 550 BCE to 330 BCE. Their capital city lay just north of Persepolis. Its most notable kings were Cyrus the Great, Darius the Great and Xerxes I. Artworks from their time show the martial and covetous nature of this empire. Many civilisations were forced to pay tribute. The Achaemenians also established their own coinage and money.

▲ Carved at Persepolis, the famous lion-bull combat is a symbol of Navroz, the Persian New Year. It represents the Earth (bull) and Sun (lion) as being equal during the spring equinox

▲ A panorama at Persepolis shows Armenian people bringing tribute to the Achaemenian king

▲ Gold ornaments show the warrior spirit of the empire

ANCICENT & MEDIEVAL ART

Oxus Treasure

About 180 pieces of jewellery, statuettes, coins and artefacts of gold and silver make up the fabulous Oxus treasure. No one knows its original owner, but the pieces belong to the Achaemenian Empire.

> **Isn't It Amazing!**
>
> The oldest carpet in the world dates from 5th–4th century BCE! The Pazyryk Carpet, found in a burial ground, is a nomad's copy of an original Persian carpet.
>
>
>
> ▲ Detail of the Pazyryk Carpet shows stylised lotus buds and fallow deer

▲ Winged sphinx at the Palace of Darius in Susa

▲ Ornate gold armlet with griffin heads and a fish-shaped vessel from the Oxus treasure

Sasanian Art

Persia rose to glory again with the Sasanian Dynasty (220–650 CE). Artists of this empire were skilled in creating decorative stone mosaics, glass, and gold and silver dishes. These were usually ornamented with animals and hunting scenes. Frescoes and illuminated manuscripts also thrived. Crafts such as carpet-making and silk-weaving became a hallmark of Persian art during this period. They were in demand far to the west and east of the world. The most striking remains of Sasanian art are seen in rock sculptures carved on steep cliffs. Famous among these are the sites of Taq-i-Bustan, Shahpur, Naqsh-e Rostam and Naqsh-e Rajab, where the victories of Sasanian rulers are shown. Sasanian artists seem to have influenced the works of Afghanistan (back then a Persian colony), where monasteries bear frescoes and huge Buddhas dating from this period.

▲ The rock art at the Naqsh-e-Rostam depicts the victory of Shahpur I over the two Roman Emperors; Valerian and philip the Arab.

▲ A boar seal of the Sasanian Era, 3rd century CE

▲ Buddhist frescoes at the monastery in Bamiyan, Afghanistan, dating from the 6th century

▲ Amazing silver and gilt vase carved with dancers and flowers

▲ Silver oval cup designed with vines and fruit

Minoa and Mycenae

The Minoans were a trading, seafaring people who lived on the island of Crete (Greece's largest island) during the Bronze Age. Their artists were exposed to ideas and materials from many lands. Their own art depicts a love for nature, particularly sea life. Around 1400 BCE, they were conquered by armies from mainland Greece. These belonged to the Mycenaeans, who brought a more martial nature to the land. The cultures of both civilisations became one. The art they left behind shows the beliefs and customs of a wealthy, pleasure-loving people.

▲ This 17th-century fresco shows seabound Minoans at the town of Akrotiri. In the distance, a lion can be seen chasing stags over the mountains

▲ This fresco shows a daredevil Minoan man grappling with a bull

◀ The Minoan Snake Goddess

▲ Marching soldiers of Mycenae

▲ The famous Vapheio Cup shows Mycenaeans capturing bulls

▲ Minoan art drew joyous inspiration from nature, as seen in this intricate gold bee

◀ Ceramic plate from Minoa shows stylised octopuses

Bull

Minoan art and sport show an affection for bulls. These animals are featured everywhere in Minoan paintings and sculptures. They are often seen with long horns and lithe, graceful bodies, leaping, or combating humans.

▶ Bull head with arching gold leaf horns

◀ Minoan bull leaper

Isn't It Amazing!

Many Greek myths and even the heroic epics of Homer—the *Iliad* and the *Odyssey*—originated in Mycenaean tales.

▲ At the Palace of Knossos, a griffon (part eagle, part lion) graces the throne room

ANCIENT & MEDIEVAL ART

Frescoes

Minoan palaces show true frescoes, called buon frescoes. These are wall paintings where colour is set on wet lime plaster. The colour is absorbed as the plaster dries. This prevents the pigments from fading away over time. *Fresco secco* is the application of colour details on dry plaster. This was used in palaces to give a three-dimensional effect to the art. The paintings were done in red, black, white, yellow, blue, and green. Men were shown with red skin and women with white. Gold was depicted with yellow, silver with blue, and bronze with red.

▶ *Minoan Women*

Jewellery

The smithies of ancient Crete refined metals such as gold, silver, bronze and even gold-plated bronze. Experts made them into jewels, often in combination with semi-precious stones, such as rock-crystal, garnet, lapis lazuli, carnelian, obsidian and jasper. The amethyst from Egypt was popular. Other materials used by jewellers included faience, enamel, soapstone, ivory, shell, and glass-paste. Most jewels were handcrafted. Some, like rings and beads, were made using moulds and casts. Gold was easily the most prized item. It could be beaten, engraved, filigreed, moulded, and punched into exquisite jewellery.

◀ A rock-crystal **rhyton** from 1500 BCE shows Minoan technique—the neck and body of the vase are joined by a crystal ring decorated with faience; the handle is made from 14 beads of gilt crystal threaded with bronze wire

▶ This hefty gold pendant is called Master of Animals. It shows a Minoan God in a field of lotus flowers. He holds a goose in each hand. The whole image is framed by what may be the horns of bulls

▶ An ornamental double-headed axe, possibly an offering to a deity

Pottery

Common forms of Minoan pottery include beaked jugs, *pyxides* (boxes), chalices and *pithoi* (giant storage jars). In later times, these evolved into the more slender floral style. Early Minoan pottery is called *Vasiliki*. It developed into pottery called *Kamares*, which used brightly coloured geometric designs on a black surface. Sea life and human figures were also seen on this pottery. Shells and flowers were sometimes carved onto it. Minoan pottery reached its zenith with the Marine style. This shows a multitude of nature, particularly sea such as octopuses, starfish, shells, sponges, coral, rocks, and seaweed. After the Mycenaean invasions, pottery developed to include the three-handled *amphorae* (a jar for wine and oil), squat *alabastra* (bottles for perfume and massage oils), goblets, and ceremonial vessels with figure-of-eight handles.

◀ The floral style shows dainty branches, with leaves and papyrus flowers. One of the most celebrated examples is the jug from Phaistos, covered entirely with reed-like decoration

▶ *Kamares pottery*

▲ Clay boxes called larnax were used to hold the dead. The larnax show paintings of cattle

Archaic, Classical, and Hellenistic Greece

Spread around the Mediterranean Sea, ancient Greece was made up of independent city-states. However, they shared the same language, religion, festivals, and culture. Most importantly, Greek artists developed their crafts and storytelling skills while Greek tyrants fell from power and one of the world's earliest democracies came to be.

Greek Art

All this is reflected in the incredible art that has influenced the world ever since. Greek artists developed their individual crafts, storytelling abilities and more realistic portrayals of human figures throughout the Archaic Period. The city of Athens witnessed the rise and fall of tyrants and the introduction of democracy by the statesman Kleisthenes in the years 508 and 507 BCE.

◀ The Stag Hunt mosaic from 4th century BCE possibly shows Alexander the Great and his companion Hephaestion

Pottery

Few ancient Greek works of wood, cloth or painting have survived the wear of time. In contrast, the sturdy fired pottery of Greece is abundant. It shows us the trends and customs of the ancient people. Colourful **mosaic** tiles also give us an idea of what Greek painting might have been like. Pottery vessels were used to store, transport and drink wine and water. Smaller jars were used for perfumes and ointments. In the 8th and 7th centuries BCE, Greek trading brought Eastern influences in pottery painting. Rigid, linear patterns gave way to Asian curvilinear styles and exuberance. Exotic animals like the lion, new motifs, and mythologies began to appear. Perhaps the best-known works are the black-figure and red-figure styles of the 7th and 6th centuries BCE. Both focus on dynamic human scenes set in high contrast hues.

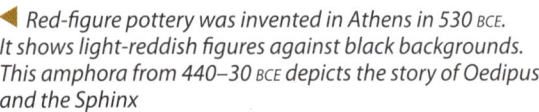

◀ The God of grape and wine, Dionysus, in a ship sailing among dolphins; black-figure pottery, 530 BCE

◀ Red-figure pottery was invented in Athens in 530 BCE. It shows light-reddish figures against black backgrounds. This amphora from 440–30 BCE depicts the story of Oedipus and the Sphinx

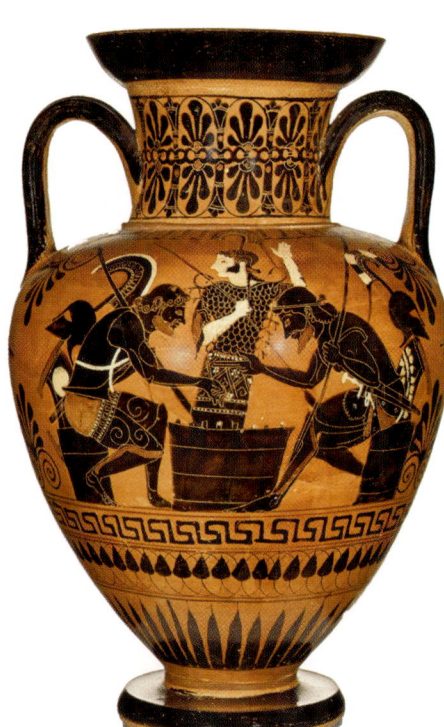

◀ In black-figure pottery, vibrant scenes of black figures were painted on strips of light surfaces and lustrous black backgrounds, as seen in this amphora depicting Achilles and Ajax playing a game during the Trojan War

ANCIENT & MEDIEVAL ART

Sculpture

The best-known figures from archaic Greece are the marble *kouros* (statue of a male youth) and *kore* (statue of a female youth). The style was influenced by Egyptian art like the statue of the Pharaoh with the goddesses. The kouros stands upright with arms at the side and one leg in front of the other. He usually has an elaborate hairstyle. These figures were often used as grave markers. A kore is draped in long fabric and jewellery, and wears a crown. During the Classical Period (480–323 BCE), such rigid sculptures gave way to more natural proportions and postures.

▲ The Great Altar of Zeus of Pergamon expresses the agony and drama typical of Hellenistic art

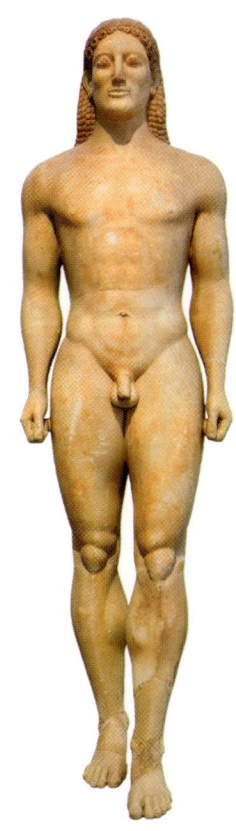

▲ The Kroisos Kouros, in Parian marble, found in Anavyssos (Greece), dating circa 530 BC, now exhibited at the National Archaeological Museum of Athens

Incredible Individuals

Timomachus is mentioned by the historian Pliny as a distinguished painter. Julius Caesar himself purchased two of his art pieces—Ajax and Medea—for the enormous sum of 80 Attic Talents. Caesar dedicated these paintings to the temple of Venus Genitrix. Though Timomachus' originals were destroyed over time, his influence can be seen in the Medea fresco at Pompeii.

► The fresco at Pompeii shows Medea. Her hand rests over a blade as she contemplates the murder of her own children, who are playing under the gaze of their teacher

◄ The Hellenistic composition titled Blinding of Polyphemus, a one-eyed Cyclops who was the son of Poseidon, the God of the sea

Art of the Roman Empire

Romans ruled such a large empire for so long that their art reflects styles from many civilisations. Roman artists imitated and adapted the best trends from the past. They also promoted art and made it available to everyone. They took visual arts to a grand scale—to fit their sense of empire. This triumphant style can be seen in coins, seals, mosaics, frescoes, and, of course, sculpture.

▲ A Roman wall painting depicting the Greek hero Hercules and Omphale, Queen of Lydia

▲ A Roman sestertius (a type of coin) engraved with the betrothal of Marcus Aurelius (who became emperor) and Faustina the Younger (daughter of the then reigning emperor)

▲ Ancient bust of Roman Emperor Antoninus Pius (c. 138–161 CE)

◀ The Ludovisi Gaul is a Roman copy of an original Hellenistic Greek sculpture

▶ The Great Cameo of France is a five-layered piece of jewellery made of sardonyx stone. This Roman artwork dates back to the 1st century CE

🏛 Painting

Inside Roman buildings of all kinds, the walls were richly and beautifully decorated. Bold colours and striking designs were used. They would often cover the wall from floor to ceiling. Designs varied from realistic and ornate subjects to imaginatively stylised works. Themes included human portraits, myths, plants, animals, and even landscapes and townscapes. Skilled artists could create an entire panorama on the walls. From the 1st century BCE onwards, a material called stucco was moulded to create three-dimensional effects and wall reliefs. This was seen in public buildings, homes, temples, tombs, and many other monuments. Painters used natural and deep shades of reds, yellows, and browns, though a number of other colours were also available. For instance, for more plain designs, blue and black pigments were preferred.

▶ A mural from the 1st-century-CE villa named House of the Vettii, in Pompeii, shows Juno, the Roman queen of gods, sitting in judgement

Roman Mosaics

A common decoration in homes and public buildings, Roman mosaics were built all across the empire. Mosaic decorated not just floors but also vaults, columns and fountains. They were made using small squares of marble, tile, glass, pottery stone or shells. Black, white and various other colours were used. Popular themes included stories from mythology, heroes, gladiator sports, hunts and nature. As with most Roman art, these often included detailed and realistic portraits of human beings as well. One of the greatest craftsmen of mosaics was Sosus of Pergamom (150–100 BCE) whose works, particularly the *Capitoline Doves* mosaic, was copied many times over for hundreds of years.

▲ A scene from the Iliad where Odysseus (Ulysses) discovers Achilles dressed as a woman and hiding among the princesses at the royal court of Skyros

◀ A mosaic from the House of the Faun, Pompeii, depicts Alexander the Great riding his stallion Bucephalus. They face the Persian king Darius III on his chariot

Sculpture

Roman sculptures can be so true to life, they even show wrinkles, scars and flabby skin! Artists preferred bronze and marble over all other mediums. Roman sculptures combined the clean lines of Classical Greek sculpture with the realism of Eastern art.

Many beautiful Roman pieces are in fact copies of lost Greek originals. In the 1st century CE, Roman sculpture became more adventurous, particularly in creating impressive light and shadow effects. This can be seen in Roman busts, portraits and funerary masks, which often show the truth of the human condition.

▲ Funerary relief of Publius Aiedius Amphio—once a slave, later a free man—and his wife Aiedia, 30 BCE

▶ The larger-than-life bronze statue of Emperor Marcus Aurelius on his stallion

◀ Roman portrait from the 1st century BCE of an elderly man with all his aged lines in realistic detail

Medieval Islam

Islam spread across the world from the 7th century onwards. In medieval times, it influenced Spain, North Africa, Egypt, Central Asia, the Middle East, and the Indian subcontinent, where it developed in unique ways.

◀ Intricate geometric and floral patterns are a hallmark of Islamic art, as seen in this detailing at the Alhambra Palace at Granada, Spain

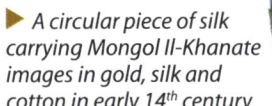

▶ A circular piece of silk carrying Mongol Il-Khanate images in gold, silk and cotton in early 14th century

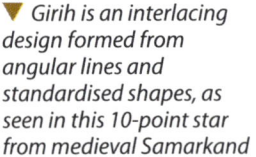

▼ Girih is an interlacing design formed from angular lines and standardised shapes, as seen in this 10-point star from medieval Samarkand

▲ A table from the Turkish Ottoman Empire showing patterned tiles on top. The side decorations are a type of inlaid veneer called marquetry

▲ Complex patterns repeat in the details and in the overall designs

Carpets

Islamic art is closely associated with sumptuous carpets used as prayer mats, wall hangings and floor covers. Warm shades of red and yellow were interwoven with black and cream to give subtle lines and bold effects. These carpets were in great demand across Europe and appear in many Western paintings. Though few carpets have survived from before the 16th century, we can see what they looked like from European paintings. The rugs that have existed till today are considered national treasures.

▲ Detail from the 16th-century Mantes Carpet of Persia, depicting animals and hunting scenes

Carvings

Elaborate carvings were popular in Islam. They were made from the same geometric and floral patterns seen in other forms of Islamic art. Carvings were made from wood, ivory, stone and crystals. They were used to ornament buildings, various types of vessels and even weaponry. Stands for the Quran, the Islamic holy book, were carved from wood.

▶ This 10th-century ivory pyxis (a medieval jewellery or cosmetic box with a separate lid) comes from Cordoba, Spain. It is carved with fierce scenes from the reign of Caliph Abd al-Rahman III and bears the name of his son Prince Al-Mughira

ANCIENT & MEDIEVAL ART

Painting

Medieval Islam was most famous for miniature paintings in books called illuminated manuscripts. Unlike other forms of Islamic art, miniatures feature human images, even of the Prophet Muhammad. The paintings can be funny, romantic, martial or philosophical. The most famous painters were a part of what is called the Baghdad School of the early 13th century. Miniatures from later periods, as from Mongol Persia, also narrated historical stories.

▲ Painting of an Arab dhow from 1225–1235

▲ A 1589 miniature in gold and watercolour shows Babur, the founder of the Mughal Dynasty, receiving a courtier

▲ An elephant-clock miniature painting from the Book of Knowledge of Ingenious Mechanical Devices by Al-Jazari, 1315

Calligraphy

Decorative writing called calligraphy is seen everywhere in Islamic art. New designs were often created using calligraphy. The content was almost always religious, most frequently about holy names and verses from the Quran.

▶ Calligraphy of the Prophet's name

▲ Golden dinars of 11th century Syria with calligraphy

Mi'raj—The Ascent of Muhammad

A Persian painting of the early 16th century called the *Ascent of Muhammad to Heaven* shows the Prophet's veiled figure surrounded by a halo of flames. This way of partially depicting the holy figure of Muhammad was conventional in the art of the Safavid Dynasty. The painting also shows Chinese influences in the shape of its figures and clouds.

▶ The 16th century Persian painting shows the veiled Prophet during Isra (the Night Journey), ascending to heaven on the back of a Buraq—a white, winged creature—in the company of angels

⊛ Incredible Individuals

One of the most skilled calligraphers and Hadith scholars of the 11th century was Fakhr-un-Nisa. Her name means 'Pride of Women'. The daughter of a scholar, she was one of the most knowledgeable people of her era. She was such a charismatic orator that people came from far-flung places to attend her sessions. After the death of her husband, the Caliph granted her a large estate, so she could continue teaching the hundreds of students who came to her. When she died at the age of 90, her funeral was held at Baghdad's Jama'e Al-Qasr and was attended by thousands of people, including scholars, students and heads of states who mourned her passing.

South Asian Art

There is a long history of beautiful art in South Asia. Bound by mountains in the north and oceans in the south, the area of modern-day Pakistan, India, Bangladesh, Sri Lanka, and parts of Afghanistan forms a geographical subcontinent. The people of this area have been united and divided at various points in history. This has led to a kaleidoscope of artistic forms, with shared themes and values. It has been primarily influenced by Hinduism, Buddhism, Jainism, Islam, Christianity, and other more local beliefs.

Indus Valley Art

The Indus Valley Civilisation was a sophisticated Bronze Age culture in what is now Pakistan and northwest India. What we know of their art comes from works of metal and clay works—vessels, figurines, and seals—which give us a clue of what these ancients were like.

▶ Seals from early Indus Valley settlements showing their hieroglyphic script

▶ The Priest-King statue is carved from soapstone and was found in the Indus Valley city of Mohenjo-Daro (Mound of the Dead)

▶ The Dancing Girl of Mohenjo-Daro

Sculpture and Engravings

On the Indian subcontinent, sculpture was the favoured medium for artistic expression. The majority of this art form is inspired by myths and legends of India. Sculptures were also a medium used by empire builders to spread tales of their conquests, and even their laws and beliefs.

◀ A pillar erected by Emperor Ashoka of the Mauryan Dynasty (321–185 BCE)

▲ Some of the finest ancient Indian sculpture comes from the Gupta Empire (319–550 CE). This 5th-century piece shows the Hindu god Krishna fighting the demon horse Keshi

Mahabalipuram

Fabulous mythological scenes cover the 7th-century cave temples by the shore of Mahabalipuram (in southern India). Among them is a relief of the all-powerful goddess Durga riding a lion and slaying the buffalo-headed demon Mahisha.

▲ In a fierce battle, Durga shoots deadly arrows at the fleeing demon Mahisha

ANCIENT & MEDIEVAL ART

The Greek Influence

Though Alexander the Great was unsuccessful in invading India, Greek styles inspired Indian artists in the north-western areas of the subcontinent. Buddha statues from this time show curly locks and drapery that are hallmarks of Greek statuary.

▶ The curly locks of the Gandhara Buddha from 1st–2nd century CE are a Greek touch to an Indian figure

◀ Engraving of a woman riding a centaur (a creature from Greek mythology) at the Sanchi stupa in central India

In Real Life

In India, precious and semi-precious stones were thought to have mystical qualities that shielded the wearer against evil forces. Among the most famous of these are the *navaratna* (nine-gem) jewels. *Navaratnas* are worn with the gems in a particular order, even to this day, for the same reason.

◀ This statue of Lakshmi, the Hindu goddess of wealth, was unearthed in Pompeii, Italy. It is proof of trade between India and Rome in the 1st century CE

Gold

India's use of gold is as old as the civilisation. In a land that was frequently fractured by the ambition of empire builders and local chiefs, systems of money were always changing. Gold offered a stable source of wealth in unpredictable times. As far back as 5,000 years ago, the Indus Valley was making beads out of the precious metal. The first widely used gold coins belonged to the Gupta dynasty around 250 CE. Since gold is in limited supply, it is frequently melted and recast into newer forms of coins, jewels and precious items. Thus, little original jewellery remains from ancient and medieval times. They can only be seen in the ancient sculptures at Bharhut, Sanchi, and Amaravati and in the paintings at Ajanta Caves. These show that kings, commoners, men, and women, all decorated themselves in a variety of gold ornaments. Indian jewellery is also described in historical literature and in the books and letters of Greek and Portuguese travellers.

◀ The golden Bimaran casket contains Buddhist relics of the 1st century BCE

▲ Kanishka, the greatest king of the Kushan dynasty, was a patron of Buddhism sometime in the late 1st or 2nd century CE. Gold coins from this time show images of Buddha and the king

 Paintings

Given the tropical climate of the subcontinent, few paintings have survived from ancient times. Most of these are on cave walls. The rest are on preserved palm leaves, where they accompany literary works. The subject of such art was religious, martial and imaginative. Some were made to appeal to warriors and rulers. They illustrated legends, romances, and histories.

▶ *Bodhisattva Padmapani from Ajanta Caves, a series of Buddhist rock-cut temples and monasteries created between the 1st century BCE and the 7th century CE*

Imperial China

The art of ancient and medieval China contains some of the most refined and delicate work ever done by humankind. It includes supremely skilled pottery, painting, calligraphy, sculpture, and jade carvings, to name just a few. Much of this art was carefully regulated by successive royal dynasties. Thus, Chinese art forms show familiar motifs that stretch across time and diverse regions.

Ritual Vessels

Shang Dynasty ritual vessels are the earliest remaining Chinese bronze work and include hemispheric pots with three legs called *ding*.

▶ Ding pots bore mask-like faces and images of tigers, cicadas, owls, rams, and oxen

◀ Chinese ritual wine server (guang) from 1100 BCE

▲ Terracotta army in the burial chamber of the First Emperor shows the power of royalty in ancient China

▲ This 26 m long 16th-century painting shows the power of the emperor. Called *Departure Herald*, it shows his luxurious ceremonial procession accompanied by his entourage, their servants, and the accompanying escort of infantry and cavalry

Painting

Chinese paintings generally used ink made of pine soot and glue. This was dissolved in a little water to get the right consistency. The artist then used a brush made of animal hair, set in finely made shafts of bamboo. Sheets of silk or paper were used for paintings. Fans, albums, vertical hanging scrolls, and horizontal hand-held scrolls (as long as 15 metres) were also painted. Since there was no way to make corrections once the ink touched the sheet, the artists had to know exactly what they were painting, and they would have to execute it with precision. Thus, Chinese artists practised to master speed, confidence, and various other techniques. Paintings were also done on dry plaster walls and screens.

Pigments

Colour was added minimally to give an emphasis but was not essential to painting as it is in other parts of the world. Bright, **opaque** pigments came from minerals—blue from azurite, green from malachite, red from cinnabar or lead, yellow from orpiment or ochre. They were used for silk-based paintings. Translucent vegetable dyes, such as blue from indigo plants, red from safflower, and green from vegetables, were used mainly for painting on paper.

◀ The 13th-century *Nymph of the Luo River* shows opaque colours used on silk

ANCIENT & MEDIEVAL ART

Calligraphy

The art of calligraphy has been considered paramount in China since the 3rd century CE. Experts believe it requires great skill and refined judgment. A person's calligraphy is also said to reveal his or her character. In most periods, the calligrapher aimed at depicting rhythm and awareness through the stroke of the brush. Rather than perception or shading, the vitality and composition were considered important.

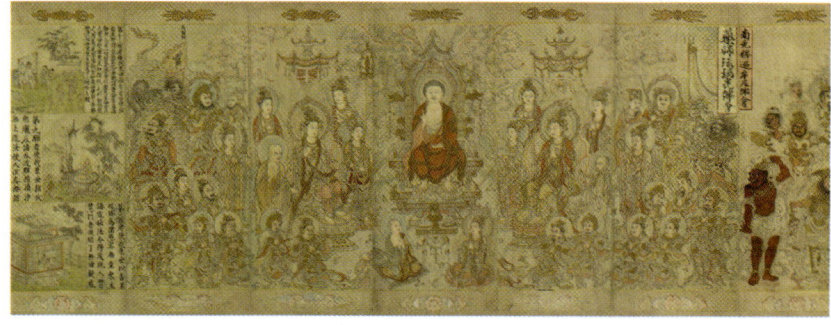
▲ *The teaching of Buddha Sakyamuni, a 12th-century painting with abundant calligraphy*

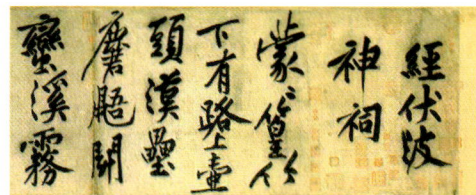
▲ *The work of renowned calligrapher Chuang Tching-tiena (1045–1105)*

▶ *This Wanli period (1573–1620) calligraphy brush is made from badger hair. The pen is decorated with two dragons in silver and gold playing with a pearl*

Pottery

As far back as the Stone Age, Chinese artists were producing exquisite painted pottery and black pottery. During the Shang Dynasty (1600–1046 BCE), high-fire stoneware and glazes were invented. During the Han Dynasty (206 BCE–220 CE), a tinted green glaze was developed in northern China. This was used in funerals as it decomposed after burial to give a silvery glow!

Celadon glazes were invented to give ceramics a fine green glaze. Celadon vessels were considered the best for drinking tea. In the 7th and 8th centuries, *sancai* (three-colour) ceramics became popular. They were covered with metallic glazes in green, yellow and brown. The bright colours mixed naturally to produce amazing effects. In the 10th century, fine white ceramics called *ding* were made and decorated with motifs from nature. The Mongol rule inspired blue and white pottery. Later, the Ming dynasty introduced more bold colours producing *wucai* (five-colour) wares.

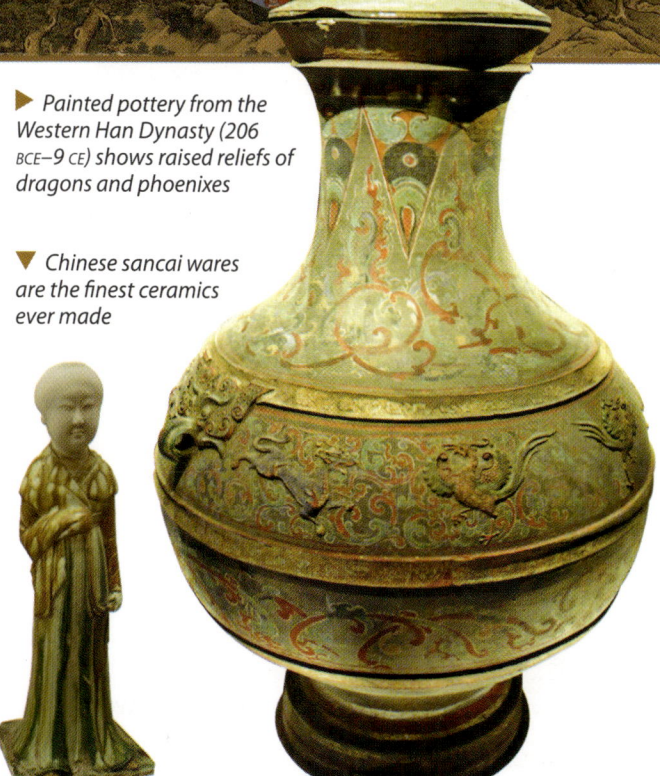
▶ *Painted pottery from the Western Han Dynasty (206 BCE–9 CE) shows raised reliefs of dragons and phoenixes*

▼ *Chinese sancai wares are the finest ceramics ever made*

Japanese Art

The earliest form of Japanese art comes from the people of the 10th millennium BCE. However, complex art is generally seen from 7th and 8th century CE onwards. This was also the time when Buddhist influences were seen in Japan. The nation's arts were sustained by imperial and noble families, as well as by shrines and monasteries. Religious art comes from Shinto, Buddhist, and Confucian beliefs. Traditionally, Japanese art is close to nature, whether in showcasing its tranquillity or its drama. The ethics of valour, humility, serenity, and beauty are abiding themes across the centuries. They can be seen in pottery, sculpture, and painting.

◀ Vessel with flame-like decorations from 3000–2000 BCE

Harvest Bells

Bronze bells (*dotaku*) of the Yayoi people were used to pray for good harvests. They were decorated with pest-fighting insects like the dragonfly, spider, and praying mantis.

▲ A bronze dotaku of the 3rd century

◀ A 12th or 13th century statue of a kami, a Shinto god

Asuka and Nara Art

Between the 6th and 8th centuries, the seat of Japanese government moved first to the Asuka Valley and then to the city of Nara. During this period, Asian influence spread throughout Japan, in particular through Buddhism. As a result, there was an explosion of art forms—particularly sculpture—that incorporated Buddhist legends and local Buddhist tales.

◀ A bronze dragon-head pitcher patterned with flying horses in gold and silver gilt. A 7th-century treasure from the Asuka period

▼ The amazing Daibutsu (giant Buddha) at the 8th-century Todai-ji temple. Each finger is as large as a person

ANCIENT & MEDIEVAL ART

Heian Art (794–1185 CE)

The nobility of the capital city Kyoto became devoted to elegant and aesthetic pursuits. The Vajrayana school of Buddhism arrived in Japan. At its centre was the worship of *mandalas*—intricate designs of the spiritual universe. These became a vital part of Japanese art. Paintings such as *raigo* (welcoming approach) were developed. These show the Buddha arriving on a cloud at the time of a person's death.

Bodhisattva

In Japan, the **bodhisattvas** Fugen Bosatsu and Monju Bosatsu are often seen in artworks as Buddha's attendants. Fugen protects devotees of the Lotus Sutra, which offers enlightenment to women. He was worshipped by Heian noblewomen.

▲ Mandala of the One-Syllable Golden Wheel in the Heian period

▲ This hanging silk scroll is a national treasure. It shows the ethereal Juichimen Kannon (Eleven-Faced Goddess of Mercy). Here, Guniyan is represented as a male bodhisattva

◀ Sculpture of Monju Busatsu, riding a roaring lion, which symbolises the voice of Buddhist law

 E-maki

Towards the end of the Heian period, horizontal hand-scrolls with paintings became popular. They were called *e-maki*. Two exquisite examples are the 1,130 illustrations of the romantic tale *Genji Monogatari* (*Tale of Genji*) and the lively 12th century *Ban Dainagon Ekotoba*, a scroll that deals with court intrigues.

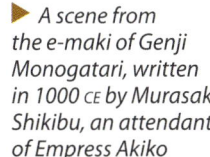

▶ A scene from the e-maki of Genji Monogatari, written in 1000 CE by Murasaki Shikibu, an attendant of Empress Akiko

Kamakura Period (1185–1333)

After the 12th century power shifted from the court nobility into the hands of warriors, the arts changed too. It now appealed to martial men. Priests who wished to spread Buddhism also chose art as a suitable medium for the teachings. Realism marked the artworks of the Kamakura period.

Muromachi Period (1338–1573)

Zen Buddhism took root in Japan at this time. Famous monks, priests and legends of Zen were the subjects of early Muromachi art. Paintings were done with quick brush strokes and minimal detail. Later on, a greater sense of space was added to paintings.

▲ Kamakura period kami artwork at the Shinto shrine Shirayama Hime Jinja

▶ A serene Muromachi guardian wearing the armour and helmet of his times

The Amazing Americas

Before Europeans came to the New World, few American languages had a word for 'art'. People who were skilled with their hands usually worked on weaponry or ceremonial pieces. This is particularly true of the more warrior-like people, such as the Incas and Aztecs. The Mayans had a heavily ritualised religion. Most of their art is focused on pleasing the gods. Thus, art served very specific purposes in the Americas.

▲ From the 8th century, a carving of King T'ah 'ak' Cha'an and two of his people

◀ The Stone of the Sun monolith (single-stone carving) is also called the Aztec calendar stone

▲ A mural of the Jade Goddess (Tlaloc Verde) at the pre-Aztec city of Teotihuacan

Nazca Lines

Geoglyphs are large lines etched into the earth. They are so vast, you can only make out the whole image from a height. The Nazca Lines of Peru are the most famous geoglyphs. They stretch over 500 sq km. Most of these images were created over 2,000 years ago by the Nazca (200 BCE–600 CE), though some are even older. The Nazca Lines generally form images of plants and animals. They include a 285-metre pelican, a 110-metre-long monkey, a 135-metre bird of prey, a 65-metre killer whale, a 50-metre hummingbird, a 46-metre spider, and various flowers and trees. Why they were drawn at all remains a mystery.

▲ Aerial view of the hummingbird

Metals and Jewels

Gold, silver and copper were the favoured metals of pre-Columbian America. Metalwork from around 4,000 BCE has been found in the Great Lakes region of North America. The earliest gold work, however, is from 1000–500 BCE. It consists of ornaments made from sheets of gold.

By the 16th century, there were well-developed technical skills in fine metalwork in Central America and the Andean regions. Craftsmen would also layer wood, bone, and shell ornaments with gold. They used jade, turquoise, rock crystal, and other precious stones with gold inlays to create exquisite pieces.

Incredible Individuals

Goldsmiths were so important in the Americas, they had their own patron deities—such as Xipe Totec in Mexico and Chibchachun in Colombia. In Peru, goldsmiths were full-time government employees, working only for the Inca. The craft and all its secrets were carefully guarded, almost like state secrets, and passed on from father to son.

▶ Deity mask of Xipe Totec

ANCIENT & MEDIEVAL ART

Regional Variation

In Mexico, bimetallic objects—usually with gold and silver—were made by a special casting process. Ecuador made a great leap in metalwork technology when they discovered a way to make complex beads of incredible fineness using an alloy of gold and platinum. It would take Europe another 500–600 years to figure out how to use platinum!

▲ Winged Runner, a Moche ornament from the 3rd–7th centuries

▲ This gold serpent—most likely Xiuhcoatl, the deity of fire—is an Aztec lip plug. Its tongue swings from side to side as the wearer walks

▲ A ceremonial knife of gold, silver, and turquoise, from 900–1100 CE

▲ A Zapotec vampire bat mosaic mask, made of 25 pieces of jade, with yellow eyes of shell

The Tomb of the Lord of Sipan

The Lord of Sipan was an ancient warrior-priest. He ruled the Moche people of Peru during the 3rd century. He was 35 or 45 years old when he passed away. The leader was buried with precious ornaments, including a mask and a large, crescent-shaped, feathered headdress. His jewellery includes necklaces, nose rings, earrings, hundreds of shell beads and a gold-and-silver sceptre. The grave also held knives, golden bells and death masks, vessels made of seashells, silver and gold rattles, and golden peanuts (an essential Moche food). A total of 451 treasured objects, and his dog, accompanied the Lord of Sipan to his afterlife.

▲ The tomb of the Lord of Sipan

Pottery

The American Indians were nomadic people for the longest time. Thus, their pottery culture began at a fairly later stage. Even then, their pottery is unlike anything seen in the rest of the world. One of the main reasons for this is that they did not use a pottery wheel. The clay was moulded or coiled and shaped with hands or on a slow turntable.

◀ Pottery from the Mayan site of Chama shows bold colours and humanised animals

◀ A clay vase modelled and painted into a music scene, from the Recuay culture (200 BCE–600 CE) of Peru

Medieval Europe

The earliest Christian arts of Europe, the Mediterranean, and Russia are called Byzantine. This art flourished from the 4th century onwards. It was influenced by the technical skills, symbols, and styles of Greece, Rome, Egypt, and Persia. During the 9th-century, religious art styles began to spread to secular areas. This period is called Romanesque. It was closely followed by Gothic art, which marked the high point of medieval art in Europe.

▲ Gothic frescoes at Elmelunde Church, Denmark

▲ The Miracle of the Child Attacked and Rescued by Blessed Agostino Novello is a painting by the talented Simone Martini (1284–1344), who spread the use of Sienese styles in Gothic art

▲ Made of gilt-bronze, the 12th-century Gloucester Candlestick is a testament to Romanesque craftsmanship

▲ From the court of Charles the Bald, Holy Roman Emperor, this plate is made of a coloured stone called serpentine rock. It is inlaid with gold fish and surrounded by 9th-century gold and cabochons (deliberately coloured gems)

Cross-cultural Byzantium

Antioch (in modern-day Turkey) was a large and influential city in Roman times. It helped form the early Christian styles that we call Byzantine art. Located along the Silk Route, Antioch was influenced by the aesthetics of the East. It adopted many oriental motifs, especially from central Asia. The Tree of Life, winged creatures of myth, rams' heads, and full front-facing portraits became common elements. Oriental Byzantine styles spread to the Eastern Orthodox Church. In Russia, it was practised until the 17th century.

Byzantine Legacy

Paintings and murals formed the bulk of Byzantine art. In particular, artwork in illuminated manuscripts spread Christian symbols across the continents. Embroidery, carvings in ivory, elaborate book covers, gold, and jewels reveal the skills of Byzantine artists and craftsmen.

▶ A pilgrim's flask from Byzantine Egypt showing 3rd century Alexandrian Saint Menas, with camels

▶ Byzantine depiction of the Archangel Michael in gold, enamel, and precious stones at St Mark's Basilica in Venice

▲ The Harbaville Triptych is a Byzantine ivory carving of Christ and the saints

Illuminated Books

In medieval times, books could only be made and copied by hand. Thus, only important subjects such as religion, medicine and governmental affairs were written down. Religious manuscripts, particularly in Islamic and Christian Europe, were decorated with gold or silver, bright colours and small beautiful pictures. These were called illuminated manuscripts. Often, the Bible's text was also artfully written with gold and silver ink on pages dyed with Tyrian purple.

▲ The birth of the Virgin Mary, from an 11th-century illuminated manuscript at the Vatican library

▲ Illuminated pages of the Homilies of Saint Gregory of Nazianzus, made during 867–86 CE, used Tyrian purple

In Real Life

Refined tableware of gold, silver, china and glass has been attractive to people ever since they were first invented. In Byzantine times, large numbers of silver plates were stamped with Christian images and used for dinner service.

▶ A 7th-century dinner plate from Constantinople with stories of David from the Bible

Medieval Icons

From the 3rd century onwards, medieval art in Europe was characterised by images of holy figures called icons, these artistic representations were worshipped by Christians. They were most often painted on wooden panels. Colours were mixed with wax and burned into the wood. Some panels were small enough to be portable. Others were used as wall hangings. Icons were also made of mosaic tiles and sculpted into metals, gems, enamel. and ivory.

Mosaics

Since Byzantine times, mosaics were used extensively to decorate walls and ceilings. Most medieval European mosaics depict religious figures. Gold tiles were a favourite, since they gave a shimmery effect. This reinforced the feeling of being in the presence of heaven. Occasionally, pagan gods, mythical beasts, and scenes from royal life would find their way into the art.

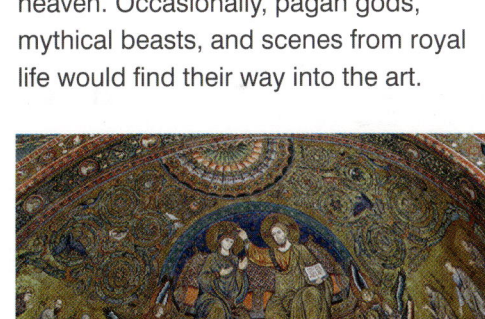

▲ The 13th-century mosaic by Jacopo Torriti shows the coronation of the Virgin with angels, saints, Pope Nicolas IV, and Cardinal Colonna. Parts of the mosaic belong to the original 5th-century work

▲ The Wilton Diptych is a rare portable 2-panel painting of King Richard II of England kneeling before the icon called the Virgin and Child. Behind him stand three saints, two of whom were previous kings of England

▲ Floor mosaic of African animals being hunted and herded found in the early Byzantine church at Mount Nebo (Memorial Church of Moses) built to commemorate the place where Moses passed away

Masterpieces of the Dark Ages

The early centuries of the medieval period are often called the Dark Ages. At this time, art was made for high-ranking priests and lords. Much of the actual work was done by monks. They were untrained men whose efforts were rarely acknowledged. Even though they created a whole new movement of art, the artists remain a mystery.

Roman Catacombs

A catacomb is a large underground cemetery where people were buried in medieval times. The Roman catacombs are decorated with some of the earliest Christian art. The paintings and mosaics here are simple. Some of them tell stories and some are symbolic. The tales express the human yearning for eternal life; to be free of death. There is the story of Lazarus who was raised from the dead by Christ, four days after his body was entombed. The tales come from both the Old and the New Testament.

▶ The Virgin and Child fresco at the Commodilla Catacomb of Rome

Symbolic Art in the Catacombs

Many Christian ideas and beliefs are painted on the catacomb walls. The sign of heaven's peace is a dove. To show immovable faith, an anchor is drawn. On the slabs of the graves, more personal symbols can be seen. For instance, an engraved tool shows you what that person's job used to be. Many symbols refer to salvation, heaven and a new life. These include the peacock, the lamb and the phoenix.

◀ The members of a family are painted above their tomb with their hands raised in prayer. The crown above the girl's head symbolises victory over death

▶ The painting of the skeleton (representing death) with an hourglass and a crown by its feet shows how death comes to all in time—even to kings

ANCIENT & MEDIEVAL ART

Bayeux Tapestry

The current Queen of England can trace her family all the way back to 1066, when Duke William of Normandy (in France) conquered England and made himself king. The story of this conquest is told in the amazing Bayeux Tapestry. This embroidered cloth is over 70 metres long. The tapestry is like a movie, with heroes, plots, action, romance, and battles. It has armies, animals, kings, knights, fortresses, ships, and many other elements. Experts think the Bishop of Odo—William's half-brother—paid for the tapestry to be created in the 1070s.

◀ *Bishop Odo rallies the troops in battle, embroidery from the Bayeux Tapestry*

Isn't It Amazing!

Early Christians believed that a peacock's flesh did not decay after death. Thus, they used the peacock as a sign of immortality.

In Real Life

Nowadays, artworks can fetch their creators thousands, even millions, of dollars. But during the Dark Ages, artist-monks received almost nothing. In contrast, the Church or State spent lavishly on the art itself. Gold (in the form of dust, foil or leaf), silver, rare gems, expensive colours and fine calf-skin canvasses were used to create masterpieces that can be admired even today.

The Apocalypse of Beatus

Beatus was an **abbot** of Libeana (in northern Spain). Around 776 CE, he wrote a masterful account of the Apocalypse—the Biblical end of the world—with multi-headed beasts, trumpeting angels and horrifically punished sinners. His *Commentary on the Apocalypse* became so popular that many monasteries made a copy of it. This was in the days when books were copied by hand. Today, 25 copies of Beatus' book exist. These were made between the 10th and 13th centuries. They vary from large and gloriously illuminated works meant for cathedrals to smaller editions for personal use.

▼ *Scenes from the early section of the Bayeux Tapestry*

▲ *The Sixth Seal by Spanish painter Magius*

▲ *The Dragon Gives His Power to the Beast, from the Beatus de Facundus (1047)*

Word Check

Abbot: A man who is in charge of an abbey of monks

Amphora: It is a long oval jar or vase with a narrow cylindrical neck and two large handles.

Bodhisattva: One who undertakes Buddhist practices that can lead them to enlightenment

Caliph: It was a title used by powerful Muslim rulers of medieval times.

Ceramics: They are clay pots that are hardened by heat, usually painted, glazed, or coloured.

Enamel: It is a glassy substance that is fused to metal (or other materials) under high heat, to give brightly coloured, glossy effects.

Equinox: Twice a year, the Sun lies directly above the equator. This is called the equinox. During the equinox, people on the equator experience equal hours of day and night.

Fresco: It is a type of mural (wall painting) in which colour is applied to wet plaster on a wall. As it dries, the wall absorbs the paint and makes it long-lasting.

Lacquer: It is a hard, shiny substance applied to wooden objects to give them a polished look.

Lapis lazuli: It is a deep blue semi-precious stone.

Mosaic: It is a form of art where the image is made by sticking together tiny pieces of coloured glass, clay, stone or other materials.

Opaque: It is an object that prevents light from travelling through, and is therefore not transparent or translucent.

Relief sculpture: They are the carvings that are made into a solid surface, like a wall or a stone slab.

Seals: They are stamps made of clay, wax, stone, or other materials. They were used to seal and stamp important documents in older times.

Standard: It is a banner or flag whose design stands for an important person or institution.

Stele: It is a tall wooden or stone slab, carved, and erected as a boundary stone, grave marker, or in memory of an important event.

Veneer: It is a thin sheet of superior wood, porcelain, or other material. It is used to cover and protect another object, like a piece of furniture.